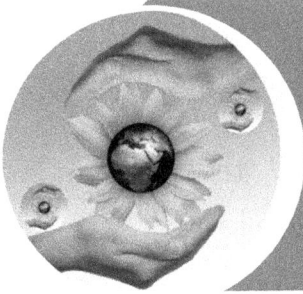

Global Competence Revisited

Alicia Su Lozeron

Introduction

GLOBAL COMPETENCE REVISITED contains a collection of Alicia Su Lozeron's articles about various topics concerning the world. In bringing global competence to the forefront, the author emphasizes a global mindset or global perspectives in achieving peace and growth for our global village.

The articles collected in this book are written with a purpose of raising global awareness about cultural sensitivity and competency. They aim to connect the world. By researching and analyzing facts as well as observing custom traditions of cross-cultural nature, Alicia Su Lozeron compels the world to observe and think critically for a more peaceful and prosperous global community.

Through her writing as well as her communication management and travel consulting company, Asia-America Connection Society, AACS 亚美合作协会, Alicia Su Lozeron has been promoting and urging global competence. Her diligence in providing quality content related to the global community has proven to be rewarding, both to her own personal fulfillment, and to the global village's needs. For herself, the work is her cause and calling. She gains a great deal of gratification through hard work and creation. For the world, her work is beneficial and educational in the ways it introduces peoples and cultures of various heritages and embraces world citizens of the global village, with their fair share of rights to being, to life, and to our magnificent Earth.

Alicia Su Lozeron's advocacy for mutual understanding and collaboration among cultures is vital for your company or personal accomplishments, on a business, cultural, educational, or entertainment dimension. Below is what readers and audiences have discerned of Alicia Su Lozeron's work:

• helps me overcome difficulties or fears and find beauty in positive human interactions;
• helps me appreciate people of various backgrounds, and expand knowledge about the world;
• helps me understand interracial or blended family relations;
• helps me savor intricate feelings and emotions about important subjects in life;

• helps me gain enjoyment through poetic narrations;
• helps me realize a new perspective of hope, courage, and respect for others;
• helps me raise awareness about cultural competence;
• helps me nurture a well-rounded global outlook;
• motivates me to promote an open/just community;
• urges me to develop the ability to see the big picture using multiple frames of references;
• helps me strengthen the ability to express genuine love;
• helps me decrease conflict by learning to trust and to resolve disagreements….

"Think Global Live Noble" -- together we can build a better world!

Works by Alicia Su Lozeron --

The Un-death of Me: Life of an Asian American Woman
(2016, A Cross-genre "Fictional Memoir")
Asia-literacy and Global Competence: Collections and Recollections
(2017, English and Chinese Versions)
Global Competence Revisited
(2019, English and Chinese Versions)

Upcoming --

A Man with Immense Love
The Un-death of Me: Life of an Asian American Woman
(Chinese Version; Japanese and Spanish Versions by Teams of Translators)

I dedicate this book to all the professionals, friends, colleagues, world citizens and travelers I have come across while exploring the world and acquiring knowledge of it. I also thank Robert Alan Lozeron, my dear husband, my love, my life-partner, and my editor who provides me with invaluable suggestions. Those who propel me to reflect on my inner self and the world appear in many facets and aspects of the articles collected in this book. They formulate the pillars of the world as I construct and understand. The factual or fictional world's intricacy lies in their existences.

With them, this book comes to life.

New York, Las Vegas, Los Angeles, Vancouver,
Toronto, London, Sydney

Asia-America Connection Society

Global Competence Revisited

Global Competence Revisited

Alicia Su Lozeron

Bigotry, nationalism, and chauvinism can only hurt. Cultivating diverse and inclusive cultures, while opening our closed minds to new ideas, on the other hand, will benefit our domestic and global communities.

Weakness creates ignorance, racism, xenophobia, and cruelty. The more self-assured you are, the more open you are to new ideas and people of different origins.

Cultural incompetence is like a shadow personality; it creeps up on you when you least expect or even realize it. When you presume and judge, you cloud your vision by having wrongful perceptions about people.

-- Alicia Su Lozeron

Content

Global Competence Revisited

1. Global Competence Revisited

The interconnected world requires our nation to nurture citizens, workers and leaders who actually know something about the world -- its cultures, customs, languages, and how the world's economic, environmental and social systems work. Taking a closer look at the concept of global competence may help illustrate how nationalism or protectionism may be counter-productive. On our path to problem solving or cultural and economic advancement, working with the rest of the world will prove to be more sensible. A global view of the big picture may just be what everyone needs to acquire or perfect.

Global competence starts with awareness, curiosity, and interest in learning about the world. While investigating the world, globally competent citizens identify, collect, and analyze credible information from a variety of local, national and international sources, including those in multiple languages. They can connect the local to the global

3

on important questions and issues. They can weigh and integrate evidence to create a coherent response that considers multiple perspectives and draws defensible conclusions.

Global competence encompasses the ability to recognize each of us has a particular perspective, and that others may or may not share the same viewpoint. One should attempt to articulate and explain others' standpoints, and further identify influences on these perceptions, including how different environments or access to knowledge, technology, and resources can affect people's ideologies. By comparing and contrasting one's perspective with others, one should be able to integrate ideas to construct a well-rounded outlook.

Globally competent citizens understand that people differ on the basis of culture, geography, faith, ideology, financial condition, and other factors, and that they may perceive different meanings from the same information. They understand how ideas should be communicated through diverse media, including through respectful online social networking and technology. They strive to interpret information as objectively as they can.

From learning about the world to making a

difference in the world takes actions and innovations. Alone or with others, globally competent citizens can envision and weigh options on evidence and insight; they can assess their potential impact, taking into account varied perspectives and potential consequences of others; and they show courage to act and reflect on their actions.

Global competence also requires the ability to understand prevailing world conditions, issues, and trends through an interdisciplinary lens, in order to understand the interconnectedness of the issue and its broad themes as well as subtle nuances. So, let's understand how the relative balance of power between societies and cultures has significant short- and long-term consequences. Let's be life-long learners.

Global Competence entails asking important questions, as well as conducting thorough examination and research before answering them.

Let's do our homework:

What are our founding fathers and leaders' teachings?

What are the principles that govern our country?

Is immigration beneficial or detrimental to our society?

Should people of particular origins be banned from traveling to our country?

Is any development such as that of the Keystone Pipeline beneficial or detrimental to our economy, and to our environment?

Global Competence entails asking important questions, as well as conducting thorough examination and research before answering them. Keeping in mind and always considering: someone else may form a completely different perspective. Only through informed dialogue and in keeping an open mind can we really be considered Globally Competent Citizens.

Before you have your answers, do more homework -- think hard and think again.

(Originally published on http://www.aacs.website/wp-content/uploads/2015/07/AACSNL2.20.17.pdf; First Printed in Asia-Literacy and Global Competence 2017)

2. Global Mindset

Achieving a global mindset is the first step towards global competence whose prevalence leads to world peace and growth. The differences of customs and traditions formulate peoples' various ideologies, and the troubles that come from the disparity indicate the focal points to problem-solving. Managing the disconnect in societies where citizens are socialized to deal with people who are like them entails development of an approach that helps them interpret and grasp their environments, as well as their ways of thinking.

A global mindset requires advancement of one's intellectual, mental, emotional and social capacity. A cosmopolitan outlook allows cognitive complexity. A habit of reflecting on one's own mind and outlook results in self-awareness and growth. A love for knowledge and diversity brings capability of empathy and self-worth. A desire for interactive discourse and human progress solidifies cultural acceptance and tolerance.

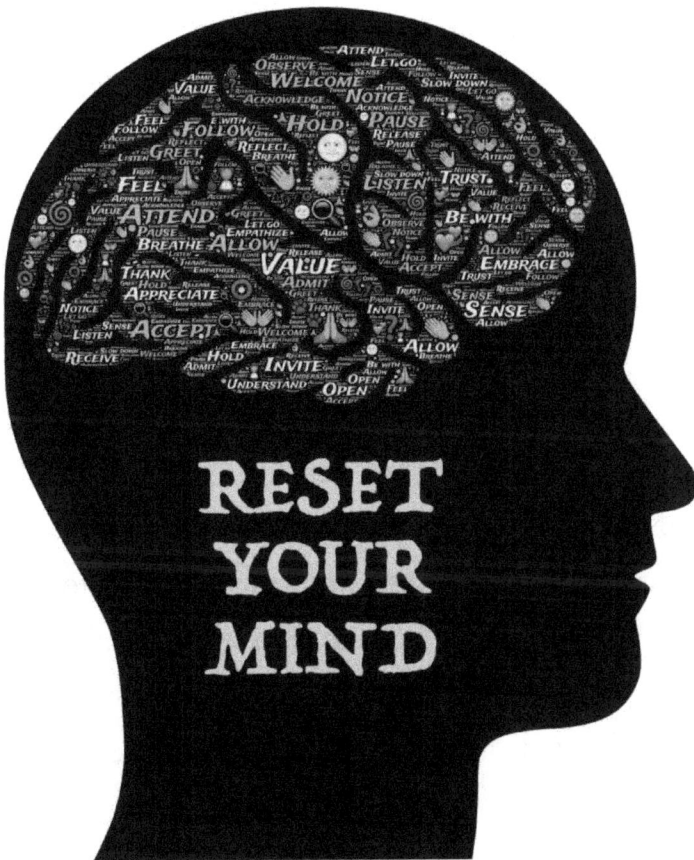

As one learns about cultures, political and economic systems, he or she reaches beyond comfort zones and nurtures a mindset that respects and appreciates others. Openness towards other cultures, other people, and other ways of living or doing things helps one adapt to new, varied and diverse universality. Exploration, then, is the opposite of blind fear or obstinacy. Only when one seeks to utilize learnings and explorations, can he or she embrace diversity and attain global competence. Without judgmental views of cultural differences, the world can become more connected, finding ways to cooperate and collaborate with their differences, instead of on their differences.

In this protectionist era, the U.S. and the U.K. increasingly seek to fight against globalization via trade wars, among other tactics. History has proven that nationalism or protectionism only leads to long-term losses. Globalization, started in the late 15th century through the expansion of global trade, and has heightened global awareness ever since. To this day, its force is unending, as manifested in China's Belt & Road initiative, which seeks to link the country with Europe and Africa. Any country averting from the globalization path will lose serious competitive advantages in the future.

Bigotry, nationalism, and chauvinism can only hurt. Cultivating diverse and inclusive cultures, while opening our closed minds to new ideas, on the other hand, will benefit our domestic and global communities.

(Originally published on
http://www.aacs.website/wp-content/uploads/2019/06/AACSNL6.5.19.pdf)

3. Global Perspective

Highly competitive and successful individuals tend to view things from a global perspective, and to reflect their own purposes while considering the big picture. It is simply short-sighted nowadays to live one's life with a parochial viewpoint. As a matter of fact, it is imperative to situate oneself globally when contemplating how one relates to his or her society as well as the rest of the world.

Embracing complex global connectivity can foster intellectual curiosity about and around the world. Through learning and understanding, one can avoid positioning oneself in stereotypical realities and identify a strategically advantageous reference frame or matrix for all. A global perspective, then, is crucial to successful global cooperation and collaboration. And it is also essential to one's wellbeing and success.

Recent elections around the world have favored anti-global rhetoric. As world powers embrace self-interests, stagnant negotiations abound. The delay of human progress reveals that looking inward or back-paddling is detrimental but ever-present. After all, the world is interconnected through business trade, through news or social media, through travel, and through political or cultural exchange. The world is more intricately interconnected than ever before.

Fear is not helping the global community or any individual/country; understanding international connections will. When an individual or a country has a global perspective, that comprehensive view will help facilitate peaceful partnerships among peoples, cultures, economies, and societies.

Expanding one's vision, outlook, and sense of "normal" toward a prolonged global perspective can indeed, enable one to see through illusive realities, reach beyond short-term benefits, establish priorities, meet challenges, find solutions, and avert problems.

4. Testing Your Own Global IQ

Global competence involves not only protocols and taboos in different countries, but also dimensions of perception that require cognizance: being open-minded, preparing for complex situations, exercising empathy and adapting to diversity.

Below is a list of statements you can test your own Global IQ with:

a. I am knowledgeable about different countries.

b. I have traveled to different countries.

c. I enjoy trying other countries' foods.

d. I am comfortable working with foreigners.

e. I am comfortable being friends with foreigners.

f. I only make friends who have the same interests as me.

g. I am retrospective, and think about my own behavior patterns.

h. I compare my own customs with others'.

i. I reflect on my own opinions.

j. I adjust my own behavior based on learnings from others.

k. I want learn more about other cultures.

l. I find other languages and ways of living intriguing.

m. I can learn things from others.

n. I have no set opinions about important issues.

o. I ask questions and research answers.

p. I like interacting with different people.

q. I listen to other people.

r. I change my opinions based on new findings.

s. I integrate various opinions and identify solutions.
t. I empathize with others.
u. I respect others.
v. I am a life-long learner.
w. There is no one ultimate way of doing things.
x. I use different measures to gauge my understanding of others.
y. I am concerned about various world issues.
z. I take actions to develop collective wellbeing of the world.

For each statement, follow the rubric below to score yourself:
Strongly Agree = 4 Points;
Agree = 3 Points;
Disagree = 2 Points;
Strongly Disagree = 1 Points

Your Global IQ Result:
Total Points 90-104 = Highly Competent
Total Points 80-89 = Satisfactorily Competent
Total Points 70-79 = Somewhat Competent
Total Points 60-69 = Inadequately Competent
Total Points 26-59 = Not Competent

5. The Importance of Developing Global Competence

Economic trends, environmental and climate changes, global crime or poverty, human rights and political struggle -- these are some of the issues we face in this interconnected world. To properly address problems or opportunities presented from globalization, it is important to become globally competent. It is important to take learned, thoughtful and planned action as a citizen of the world.

One must investigate the world from various perspectives, engage in discourses and take actions to attain global growth. Understanding one's own environment entails acquiring new skills to adapt to the ever-changing world. Every decision and action has far-reaching effect on different parts of the world. It is everyone's responsibility to sustain, to innovate, and to make a difference, regardless of one's individual goals and objectives.

Global competence means to learn, to think and to proactively take action using worldly knowledge and skill. This kind of capacity and character is crucial for success and wellbeing of any individual or country. When the world can exercise critical thinking, rational reasoning, positive outlook, innovative approach, cultural understanding, empathy and sensitivity, then, cooperation and collaboration can take place to help build relations, solve problems and create new opportunities.

Global competence involves a realization: knowledge is not finite; continual learning and exploration is required. Viewing the world from complex and divergent perspectives can create alternative solutions and realities, including a new heightened level of compromise. Navigation of the world for individuals or countries with global competence will become easier and more productive. Because they understand how local issues are connected with bigger issues in the world. They recognize every little choice they make may have global repercussions. They know it is vital to support government, corporate, or nonprofit missions that drive sustainability across the world. They are responsible and careful when it comes to social media. "Think Global, Live Noble." Work with others to make a better world!

6. Deconstructing the Migration Lexicon

A person who works or lives outside his/her country is an expatriate, or expat for short. Originated from the Latin terms ex ("out of") and patria ("country, fatherland," "expatriate" or "expat" is defined regardless of one's skin color or country of origin. However, "expat" exclusively applies to white people. The migration lexicon readily implies hierarchy and prejudice.

In reality, color draws a line for the usage of the word. Instead of being called "expats," Africans are immigrants. Arabs are immigrants. Asians are immigrants. Living/working temporarily or permanently outside one's native country does not determine whether one is labeled as an expat or an immigrant; his/her skin color may contribute to his/her label. This happens everywhere -- in the US, and in Hong Kong, for example. In the US, top African professionals and Asian global developers, to name a few, are not expats like Europeans; they are "highly qualified immigrants." In Hong Kong, Westerners are considered expats; Filipino domestic helpers are visitors; Mandarin-speaking Chinese are "Mainlanders."

Taking a closer look, one can discern that race is not the only factor that governs the label of an "expat" or "immigrant." More precisely, country of origin, social class, or economic status also determines how people who live abroad are regarded. Some people are described as expats, others as immigrants, and some simply as migrants. This supremacist ideology is outdated and unjust. The world needs to be aware of it, and the deconstruction of this worldview must be undertaken.

There were 258 million international migrants in 2017, according to a UN report. The number is growing rapidly, from 173 million in 2000, 222 million in 2010, and 244 million in 2015. It is a growing trend, and living abroad allows a great opportunity for people to become globally competent world citizens. While some of the so called "expats" stay in their privileged living quarters and demand English menus in restaurants wherever they go, they fail to acquire foreign languages, understand different countries' peoples or cultures.

An expat is someone who moves to another country for work without the intentions of becoming a permanent resident or citizen of the country, and an immigrant is someone who moves to another country with the intention of permanently living there and/or becoming a citizen of that country. Race, income, status, and privilege should not be the indicators for us to judge either term. Most people move overseas in hopes of bettering their lives. When one lives abroad, it is a fabulous opportunity to learn, to adjust, and to be assimilated to a new society. Perhaps keeping an open mind to discover and absorb, is the very first step one can take to deconstruct the migration lexicon. As an expat, immigrant, or migrant, one's moving and living abroad experience is enhanced when he/she can freely enjoy life and the new community without borders. A globally competent world citizen would embrace this opportunity.

(Originally published on http://www.aacs.website/wp-content/uploads/2018/08/AACSNL8.5.18.pdf)

7. Ways to Develop Global Competence

To react productively to situations in the global community requires the ability to make best use of the interconnected world resources without losing one's sense of identity. In other words, one needs to exercise global competence and find a position in the most beneficial conditions on individual, national and international levels. Considering one's own cultural beliefs and partialities while comparing with other global views and components from other cultures, marks the crucial groundwork in making globally competent decisions and choices.

Other than staying reflective, retrospective and open to new ideas, one can take specific actions to attain global competence. For example, learn another language or study another culture. Travel or live abroad. Be immersed in various cultures. Communicate and discuss ideas with peoples of diverse backgrounds. Acquire interdisciplinary knowledge and skills. Develop wide-ranging interests and hobbies. Use the internet and technology responsibly and effectively. In using new found knowledge and experience, one is able to make a difference for the world -- one is being globally competent. People who look outward and upward tend to have broader and deeper visions for a better world.

Awareness of self and one's surrounding allows for a well-rounded global perspective. In turn, this awareness propels curiosity, openness, flexibility, adaptability, and leads to healthy and constructive interactions. Ask questions, reach out, research, observe, analyze, interact, synthesize, empathize, understand, evaluate, relate, connect, and learn from one another. Learn from exploration and investigation. Continual learning and growth will occur when one seeks to flex and share practices of effective cooperation and collaboration. And, when minds are ready for harmony and progress, opportunities will present themselves in balanced contexts. People, then, can work together to resolve issues, build trust and respect, and promote global peace and prosperity.

8. Starting Over with New Year Resolutions

People around the world like to make new-year resolutions: lose weight, stop drinking, quit smoking, become more active, and engage in a new hobby, etc. Notably, the tradition of new-year resolutions came from four millennia ago, far older than the establishment of the festival.

When the Babylonians made the historic first resolutions, they often had practical agricultural or economic concerns -- like repaying debts or returning borrowed farm equipment to receive harvests bestowed by the gods. Akitu, a 12-day festival to celebrate the renewal of life, kicked off the agrarian year. Similar in mindset, the ancient Egyptians wished for good fortune and abundance, making sacrifices to Hapi, the god of the Nile, at the beginning of their year in July when the Nile's annual flood started a fertile period.

Emperor Julius Caesar designated January 1st New Year's Day, naming the month of January after Janus, the god of beginnings and endings. The Romans prayed and confessed in order to reinforce their values and beliefs.

1. Delete Hate 2. Practice Tolerance

3. Demand Wisdom *Resolution* 4. Remember Compassion / Empathy

5. Replace Fear with Love

Modern-day new-year resolutions have lost their religious implications, but maintain the cleansing/

catharsis overtones. Today, we still like to have a clean slate around the New Year's. New-year resolutions are common in countries like America, Canada, England, Wales, Scotland, Northern Ireland, Australia, and South Africa, while Latin American, Scandinavian, Asian and Eastern European countries have their own versions of festivities.

In Poland, New Year's Eve is "St. Sylvester's Eve" because Pope Sylvester captured a dragon and prevented the doom of the world. Estonians eat 7, 9, or 12 times on New Year's Eve, but leave some food for the dead ancestors and spirits who come visit on New Year's Eve. In Bosnia and Herzegovina, people prepare fireworks, go to concerts, and give gifts from *Dyed Mraz* (Father Frost) for the kids. Russians' new-year resolutions often focus on education. The Chinese/Korean New Year is between January 21st and February 20th according to the lunar calendar. People wear new clothes to start the year fresh.

From ancient to modern days, from the East to the West, the beginning of the year is the time to celebrate and to set important goals. Universal hopes and dreams often relate to good health, love, career, finance, and education. No matter how one led his or her life before, a better self or way of living is in the making!

(Originally published on
http://www.aacs.website/wp-content/uploads/2018/01/AACSNL1.5.18.pdf)

9. What the World Learns from Chinese New Year Celebrations

Chinese New Year celebrations are used to scare away the mythical wild beast Nien (年, which also is the word for "year"). Legend has it that at the end of each year, Nien appears and pillages human towns and villages. Therefore, loud firecrackers and bright lights are meant to shoo the beast or evil spirits away, and the 15-day New Year festivities have taken roots as the most important of Chinese traditions.

According to the lunar calendar, Chinese New Year usually falls in between the end of January and mid-February, and is celebrated in Asian countries such as China, Taiwan, Singapore, Hong Kong, Vietnam, Korea, and Japan, as well as among the Chinese people in Thailand Indonesia, Brunei, Malaysia, and around the world. Family and friends gather to feast and observe traditional rituals. Listed below are some important customs.

Red Couplets bearing auspicious characters or phrases, as well as red décor such as lanterns, Chinese knots, potted kumquats and golden orange trees adorn every street, storefront and home. The color red is ubiquitous, because it is associated with wealth and good fortune in Chinese culture. House Cleaning before the Chinese New Year is also customary. Windows are scrubbed, floors are washed and furniture is dusted in preparation for the New Year, ridding the bad luck of the past year. However, dusting is avoided on New Year's Day, lest that good fortune be swept away.

As the New Year approaches, various activities keep people busy and jolly. New Year's Markets sell decorations, red envelopes, toys, clothes and trinkets. Families shop, decorate their houses, and wear new clothes on the Chinese New Year. Many people also pray at the Temple on the third day of the New Year.

Red envelopes, called "hong bao 红包 " in Mandarin, are filled with small or hefty amounts of money and placed underneath pillows of children or unmarried/jobless young adults on the Chinese New Year's Eve. Hong Bao money is to suppress the Nien (Ya Sui 压岁), while the red color denotes good luck/fortune and happiness/abundance in the Chinese Culture.

The Chinese New Year's Eve meal "Tuan Yuan Fan 团圆饭," is the most important dinner of the year. Typically, families gather at a designated relative's house or a restaurant for dinner on the Chinese New Year's Eve. During each day of the 15-day celebration, families rotate gatherings in homes of their relatives. Married daughters return to their maternal families on January 2nd of the Lunar Calendar (Hui Niang Jia 回娘家), and the festivities are day-long, with many red envelopes given or received. The traditional foods are:

- Eight Treasures Rice (contains glutinous rice, walnuts, different colored dry fruit, raisins, sweet red bean paste, jujube dates, and almonds);
- "Tang Yuan" -- black sesame or small glutinous rice ball soup; or a Won Ton soup;
- Fish -- The tradition of eating fish during the New Year stems from the fact that the Chinese word for "surplus" or "profit" (余) sounds the same as the word for fish (鱼). Thus, it is believed that eating fish will bring wealth, and every year, there will be surplus wealth/fish (Nian Nian You Yu 年年有余/年年有鱼).

- Dumplings are shaped like the old Chinese money Yuan Bao 元宝, and symbolize wealth.
- Chicken, Duck, and Pork Dishes;
- Mandarin Oranges symbolize good fortune.
- "Nian Gao" or "Song Gao", literally translates to "loose cake"- which is made of rice which has been coarsely ground and then formed into a small, sweet round cake.

As descendants of dragons, Chinese perform **Lion or Dragon Dances** on the streets with nonstop rhythms of drums and cymbals, firecrackers, and exchanges of "Gong Xi Fa Cai" (恭喜发财 Congratulations on your wealth and prosperity). On the fifth day of the New Year when many people have to return to work, Dancing Dragons/Lions perform in the front of businesses and office buildings to bring good fortune.

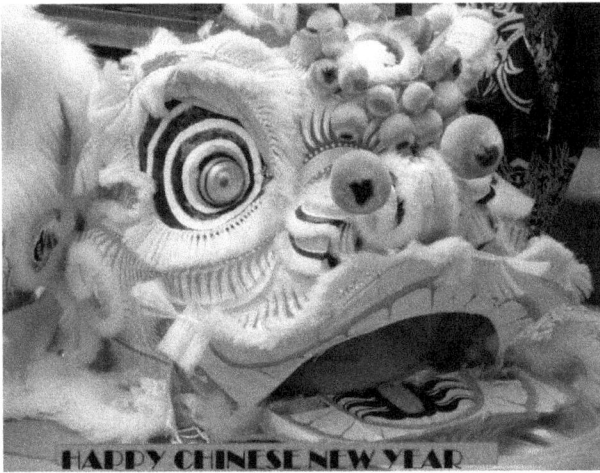

HAPPY CHINESE NEW YEAR

The 15th day of the New Year is known as **The Lantern Festival** "Yuan Xiao Jie" (元宵节), which marks the end of the Chinese New Year celebrations. All types of lanterns are lit throughout the streets; poems and riddles are often written for entertainment. Paper lanterns are also created on wheels in the form of the animal of the year. Lion and Dragon Dances are performed everywhere again to bring the New Year celebrations to a grandiose end, whereas people send their wishes along with the lanterns to the heaven, hoping for a safe and successful new year.

What can the world learn from Chinese New Year celebrations -- or, from any holidays or festivals? A sense of cultural festivity and identity, like the one characterized during the Chinese New Year, can help individuals or nations attain self-awareness and self-respect to be better situated in the global community. To embrace one's traditions and customs is the first step towards a healthy and constructive mindset. With self-awareness or self-respect, the world can hope to advance further!

(Originally published on http://www.aacs.website/wp-content/uploads/2018/02/AACSNL2.4.18.pdf)

10. When the World Celebrates Independence Days

Americans celebrate 4th of July Independence Day with fireworks, barbecues, parades, and concerts, decorating everything in red, white and blue. The holiday marks the signing of the Declaration of Independence on July 4th, 1776, and signifies the hard won freedom that makes quintessential America. Likewise, patriotic traditions around the world indicate significant spirits of different countries, with intriguing historic stories behind.

Canada Day, July 1st

Canadians use red and white maple-leaf flag colors to decorate parades, carnivals, picnics, while fireworks and Snowbirds (military planes demonstrating aerobatics) highlight celebratory acts.

France, July 14th Bastille Day

France commemorates July 14th the Bastille Day

when, in 1789, Parisians broke into the Bastille fortress to release prisoners and catalyzed the French Revolution that ended the country's tyrannical oppression. A military parade on the Champs Elysees starts the celebration of this significant holiday; fireworks over the Eiffel Tower are also lined up with parties, galas and good times.

Indonesia, August 17th

Indonesia proclaimed its independence in 1945 and fought for its freedom with the Netherlands until 1949. **Panjat pinang is the celebratory** game that demonstrates Indonesian determination. During this game, oiled-up tall nut trees carry buckets of prizes at the top, and young men work together, using each other's bodies as step stools, to clamber to the top to retrieve the prizes.

Cambodia, November 9

In 1887, Cambodia was made part of the unified colony of French Indochina, until World War II, when the country fell under Japanese control. It was returned to France after the war, and then finally gained its independence on November 9, 1953. Cambodians celebrate their freedom with parades, cultural events and fireworks.

India, August 15th

East Indians celebrate the ending of 200 years of British colonial rule in 1947 by flying kites that carry images of the Indian flag.

South Korea, August 15th

Gwangbokjeol (literally "Restoration of Light Day") is the name of the South Korean independence day. On this day, special prison pardons are given to commemorate the freedom spirit.

South Africa, April 27

South Africa declared its independence from Britain on May 31, 1910, and celebrates April 27th as "Freedom Day." On April 27, 1994, the first democratic, non-racial elections were held and Nelson Mandela was voted president. This day marks the end of colonialism and apartheid, and is celebrated with parties, inspirational speeches, and braais (barbecues).

Mexico, September 15 - 16

Mexicans take to the streets to memorialize the Grito de Dolores, the battle cry of the Mexican War of Independence with Spain, won in 1810. From the 15th to the 16th, parades, food, concerts, and fireworks last for two days.

Peru, July 28 and **29**

Peruvians toast to freedom with a classic national drink Pisco Sour. Cannon salutes and parades along with colorful costumes, drum beats commemorate the date when Jose de San Martin proclaimed Peru's independence from Spain in 1821. July 29 serves as a day to honor the Armed Forces and National Police.

Of the 196 countries in the world, <u>90% of them became independent after 1800</u>. Eastern European countries had long struggles with Russia, Central/South Americans with Spain, and Asians or Africans with British, Dutch, Japanese or other colonial powers. Independence days are often attained in hard fought battles to claim freedom, whereas some national holidays commemorate a significant day in the history of the country, or the birth of a national hero who helped establish the country's independence. They symbolize major historic development and progress of national histories -- certainly noteworthy.

(Originally published on
http://www.aacs.website/wp-
content/uploads/2018/07/AACSNL7.1.18.pdf)

11. How the World Celebrates Halloween

Halloween, one of the world's oldest holidays, is celebrated today in various countries around the globe. In **the United States and Canada,** 65% of the population decorates homes and offices for Halloween, a percentage only second to Christmas. Adults and children alike, revel in celebrations derived from ancient festivals and religious rituals, including costume parties, jack- O'-lanterns carved out of pumpkins, trick-or-treating, pranks and games.

In **Ireland**, the Spirits of Meath Halloween Festival in County Meath is the origin of Halloween. An ancient Celtic festival we now know as Halloween started more than 2,000 years ago. Nowadays throughout the country, Halloween is still welcomed with bonfires, party games, and traditional food, such as barmbrack, an Irish fruitcake that contains coins, buttons, rings and other fortunetelling objects. (If a young woman gets a ring that has been baked in a pastry, bread or any kind of food, she'll be married by next Halloween. A straw means that a prosperous year is ahead.) After trick-or-treating, most people attend parties where many games are played, including "snap-apple," a game in which an apple on a string is tied to a doorframe or tree and players attempt to bite the hanging apple. In addition, treasure hunts for candy or pastries and card games are also popular, and of course drinking and feasting.

Once upon a time, **English** children made "punkies" out of beetroots and carried their "punkies" through the streets while singing the "Punkie Night Song." They knocked on doors and asked for money. Turnip lanterns were placed on gateposts to protect homes from the spirits who roamed on Halloween night. Another custom was to toss objects such as stones, vegetables and nuts into a bonfire to frighten away the spirits. These symbolic sacrifices were also for fortune-telling. If a pebble burned and became invisible in a fire pit, the person who tossed the pebble would not survive another year. If nuts exploded in the blaze, lovers would quarrel and have troublesome marriages. However, the English ceased celebrating Halloween with Martin Luther's Protestant Reformation. Since followers of the new religion did not believe in Saints, they stopped celebrating the Eve of All Saints' Day. On the other hand, a new autumn ritual did emerge. **Guy Fawkes Day** festivities were to commemorate the execution of a notorious English traitor, Guy Fawkes. (On November 5, 1606, Fawkes was executed after being convicted of attempting to blow up England's parliament building.) Children walk the streets carrying an effigy or "guy" and ask for "a penny for the guy."

In **Austria**, people leave bread, water, and a lamp on the table before retiring on Halloween night, because such items would welcome the dead souls back to earth. The **Belgians** believe that it is unlucky for a black cat to cross one's path and also unlucky if it should enter a home or travel on a ship. They light candles in memory of dead relatives. In **Germany**, people put away their knives on Halloween night to prevent the returning spirits from being harmed. In **Czechoslovakia**, chairs are placed by the fireside on Halloween night, one chair for each living family member and one for each family member's spirit. In **Sweden**, Halloween known as "Alla Helgons Dag," is celebrated from October 31 until November 6.

In Mexico, Latin American countries and Spain, Día de los Muertos -- the Day of the Dead/All Soul's Day -- honors deceased loved ones and ancestors. It takes place on November 2, commemorated with a three-day celebration that begins on the evening of October 31. Altars are constructed in homes to honor deceased relatives. Skull-shaped candies, flowers, photographs, samples of the deceased's favorite foods and drinks, and fresh water are offered. Also, a wash basin and towel are prepared so that the spirit can wash before indulging in the feast. Candles and incense are burned to help the deceased find the way home. Families also tidy the gravesite of their deceased relatives, snipping weeds, making repairs, painting, and decorating. On November 2, relatives gather at the gravesite to picnic and reminisce. Feasts, lots of tequila, dancing and mariachi music, as well as parades of people dressed as skeletons, all ensure that one's ancestors are honored.

Other than the imported Halloween celebrations, Asia has its way of paying tributes to the ghosts. In **China and Taiwan**, April is the month to honor people's ancestors, whereas the Hungry Ghost Festival /Zhongyuan Festival (中元节) is on the 15th day of the 7th lunar month. The whole month of July starting from the seventh day, is dedicated to dealing with ghosts and worshiping ancestors. Festivities include parades, operas, burning incense, food for the dead and performances to entertain the spirits. The **Japanese** celebrate the "Obon Festival" in July or August (also known as "Matsuri" or "Urabon") in dedication to their ancestors' spirits. Special foods and bright red lanterns are prepared.

Candles are lit and placed into lanterns which are then set afloat on rivers and seas. In **Korea**, "Chusok" in August is for families to thank their ancestors. They make offerings of rice and fruits at their ancestors' graves.

Halloween, incorporating all the best superstitions of the Roman, Celtic, Catholic and European folk traditions, has become a celebration of the human spirit and the afterlife. While Christmas elicits good cheer, Halloween fosters a night of sensory stimulation. A day to cast out evil spirits as well as celebrate the dead, Halloween is favored and rejoiced around the world.

(Originally published on http://www.aacs.website/wp-content/uploads/2015/07/AACSNL10.15.17.pdf)

12. How the World Celebrates Christmas

Christmas season is the one time of year that people simply like to celebrate locally. Family members tend to gather in their hometowns and revel in one another's company. However, Christmas festivities can be very exotic. There are various Christmas traditions around the world, fascinating and fun.

People in **Iceland** often exchange books on Christmas Eve, then read them and eat chocolate the rest of the night. The tradition is called Jolabokaflod, or "The Christmas Book Flood." Iceland publishes more books per capita than any other country.

Greenland's traditional Christmas dish, *kiviak*, takes seven months to prepare. Hollowing out a seal skin and stuffing it with 500 auks/sea birds to ferment, people feast straight from the seal when the holiday rolls around.

On Christmas Day, **Lebanese** children go up to any adult and say, "Editi 'aleik!" ("You have a gift for me!"). **Syrian** children receive gifts from one of the wise men's camels, the youngest and smallest in the caravan, who fell down exhausted at the end of the long journey to Bethlehem.

Christmas traditions in African countries such as **Kenya** and **Uganda** are much more religious and less commercial. Stones, leaves, and other natural items as birthday presents for Jesus are collected. Roasted goats are prepared for Christmas feasts, while **South Africans** feast on a seasonal delicacy -- the deep-fried caterpillars of Emperor Moths!

Ethiopia follows the ancient Julian calendar, so Ethiopians celebrate Christmas on January 7. The Ethiopian Orthodox Church's celebration of Christ's birth is called Ganna. Everyone dresses in white and attends church. Twelve days after Ganna, on January 19, Ethiopians begin the three-day celebration called Timkat, commemorating the baptism of Christ.

In many regions in **France**, Christmas celebrations start with St Nicholas day on the 6th of December. On Christmas Eve, children put their polished shoes out in front of the chimney and hope that '*Père Noël*' (Father Christmas) fills the shoes with sweets. In **the United States and England**, children hang stockings on their bedpost or near a fireplace on Christmas Eve, hoping that it will be filled with treats while they sleep.

A manger scene is the primary decoration in most southern European, Central American, and South American nations.

In **Italy**, a nativity scene, a '*presepe*', is usually put up in churches, town squares, and often in houses. '*Babbo Natale*', Father Christmas, hands out presents to children on Christmas Day, but gifts are exchanged only on January 6, the day of Epiphany.

Spain begins celebrating the Christmas season on December 8 with a weeklong observance of the Feast of the Immaculate Conception. Evergreens decorate the churches and outdoor markets, while tambourines, gourd rattles, castanets, and miniature guitars are for sale to enliven the singing and dancing in the streets. Children go from house to house reciting verses or singing carols for treats or gifts.

In the **Philippines**, a Christmas lantern called '*parol*' is designed in the shape of a star, in remembrance of the star of Bethlehem, and mainly made out of bamboo and paper.

In the weeks up to Christmas, **Australians** join in Christmas picnics organized by various churches and sing Christmas carols on the beach. People come together at night to light candles and sing Christmas carols outside. A jovial Southern Hemisphere Christmas it is!

Whether in the North, South, East, or West, a Christmas/pine tree, a manger, mistletoe, a poinsettia, a specific food, or a family tradition, the

Holiday Spirit is strong in many cultures and places around the world and inspires joy, hope, and love. Christmas traditions may be diverse; Christmas joviality is certainly universal!

(Originally published on http://www.aacs.website/wp-content/uploads/2017/12/AACSNL12.7.17.pdf)

13. Observing Asia as a VIP in World Economy

Asia's rising affluence has been attracting the world's private banks to tap into its markets. For example, <u>France's second largest bank, Credit Agricole SA</u>, has been expanding its presence in the region. Julius Baer Group Ltd., Switzerland's third-largest publicly traded private bank, has grasped Asia's huge growth potential, and foresees a third of its business to be coming from the Asian continent.

Chief Executive Officer Boris Collardi indicates that Asia currently accounts for about 20 percent to 25 percent of its business. He forecasts Asia's potential to overtake Europe as Julius Baer's biggest revenue-generating region. The bank has been hiring extra staff to meet Asian market needs, and will continue to recruit in Asia. Adding more hubs in the region has become necessary.

Julius Baer, the fifth-largest private bank in Asia, had $82.4 billion in assets under management and 380 relationship managers at the end of 2016. The numbers keep increasing. Regional competitors DBS Group Holdings Ltd. and Oversea-Chinese Banking Corp., which have expanded via acquisitions, are close behind in sixth and seventh, according to Asian Private Banker.

Meanwhile, Boston Consulting Group predicts that Singapore and Hong Kong will attract wealth from abroad at more than twice the speed of

Switzerland. As Asia's economic expansion draws cash from millionaires, offshore assets will rise at a compound annual average rate of 8 percent through 2021 in Singapore. Hong Kong's will climb 7 percent, and Switzerland's, 3 percent. Switzerland remains the world's No. 1 offshore wealth management hub with $2.4 trillion in assets, twice as much as Singapore's.

"Relative to Switzerland, Hong Kong and Singapore are growing faster because of the economic growth from China to India," said Mariam Jaafar, a Singapore-based BCG partner. "In clients' minds, Singapore is more independent and secure. The government is also very supportive of the wealth management industry." China's restrictions on investment outflows may slow some of the movement of assets from the nation, Jaafar suggested. Still, China ranks above Taiwan, and Hong Kong and Indonesia are the largest source of offshore wealth in the Asia-Pacific region.

Banks from UBS Group AG to Credit Suisse Group AG and DBS Group Holdings Ltd. have been adding wealth management staff to service global clients. Offshore assets in private banking hubs worldwide grew almost 4 percent in 2016 to $10.3 trillion, based on BCG's report. Amidst the wealthy and rich, Asia certainly plays a VIP role, and requires special attention when one seeks globally competent and strategic positions.

(Originally published on http://www.aacs.website/wp-content/uploads/2015/07/AACSNL9.17.17.pdf)

14. Challenges of
Our Global Community

Global cooperation and collaboration has its highs and lows. The challenges of international development require collective planning and action on issues that affect the world as a whole. Countries must work together to tackle challenges for our global community.

Humanitarian Crises vs. Sustainable Peace

The <u>Universal Declaration of Human Rights</u> in 1948 did not prevent 71 countries from suffering net declines in political and civil liberties according to <u>data</u> from the UN. Global freedom or gender equality still requires attention. We need to address global and local inequalities, and at the same time protect human rights around the world.

As a matter of fact, polarization and inequality represent significant threats to sustainable peace. The UN and France's G7 summit aim to tackle sustainable development along with healthcare coverage, while human conflicts and natural disasters continue to impede development, security and peace worldwide. Conflicts in Syria, Colombia, and the Democratic Republic of the Congo have caused 20 million displaced people. Further, problems in Nigeria, Somalia, South Sudan, and Yemen continue to cause displacement. Approximately 132 million people need humanitarian assistance today, at an estimated minimum cost of $21.9 billion.

Climate Change

Greenhouse gas emissions <u>continue to rise</u>. We have witnessed disastrous tornadoes, floods and fires that destroy families, harm livelihoods, and generally create havoc. Reduction of global warming to stay within 1.5°C above pre-industrial levels is necessary. The UN's <u>Climate Summit</u> opens in September 2019 and highlights transition to a low-carbon economy. Meanwhile, the <u>IPCC</u> (the Intergovernmental Panel on Climate Change) seeks to publish two scientific reports on critical climate issues. Along with the UN, G20 Summit in Japan and G7 Summit in France earlier in the year feature critical climate actions.

Financing Development

We need to direct private capital towards building sustainability and resilience, re-invest in poor and war-torn areas, and regulate investment incentives and risks. The UN works with agencies and Member States, as well as the private sector and civil society to finance result-driven development.

Modernization of the UN

The UN's elements of reform are: peace and security, management, and the development system. Their aim is to identify and implement ideas and actions and influence the world in a positive fashion. New organizational changes are in place as outlined by the <u>UN</u>:

- Peace and Security Restructuring: two new departments (Department of Political and Peacebuilding Affairs and Department of Peace Operations) to focus on preventing conflict and sustaining peace;
- Management Reform: two new departments (Department of Management Strategy, Policy and Compliance and Department of Operational Support) to support the delivery of UN mandates.

Political and economic unrest, human conflict, climate change, and inequalities continue to impair our global community. Collective action across nations is vital to overcome today's challenges, and notably, grassroots movements of global citizens are indispensable. Requirements from the private sector are essential to provide strong support for global cooperation and collaboration. Indeed, people and partnerships set the foundation of global progress. We must embrace our global community, new ideas, and uphold our individual efforts to help with globally interconnected challenges.

15. Deliberating Facts vs. Opinions

Fake news has the potential of swaying ideologies and beliefs. The line between facts and opinions can be blurred, while statements taken out of their contexts to serve political purposes. Such manipulation of text or data is worrisome particularly when some are willful in skewing media news and reports. The Pew Research Center conducted a survey that showed only 26% of Americans can distinguish between facts and opinions in news. Therefore, it becomes crucial to have tools for tracking how "alternative facts" spread, and for identifying fake stories to block them altogether. While stronger regulatory rules need to be in place, Facebook, Google and big media companies are making baby-steps efforts to stop the spread of fake stories and news reports.

With only a quarter of our population savvy in discerning biased or fake news, the responsibilities of educating the public also lie in "<u>the politically aware, digitally savvy and those more trusting of the news</u>."

> 36% of Americans with high levels of political awareness (those who are knowledgeable about politics and regularly get political news) correctly identified ... factual news statements, compared with about half as many (17%) of those with low political awareness. Similarly, 44% of the very digitally savvy (those who are highly confident in using digital devices and regularly use the internet) identified ... statements correctly versus 21% of those who are not as technologically savvy. And though political awareness and digital savviness are related to education in predictable ways, these relationships persist even when accounting for an individual's education level.

Once again, individual efforts are called for making our community a safer and better place.

Partisan affiliations also influence how Americans differentiate between factual and opinion statements. Both Republicans and Democrats show a propensity to favor statements that appeal to their own political interests. In other words, they label both factual and opinion statements as factual to rationalize, justify, or solidify their own political side. <u>Knowing the difference between facts and opinions</u> is then, the first step to raise awareness about the fact/opinion dynamics:

A **fact** is a statement that can be proven true or false. An **opinion** is an expression of a person's feelings that cannot be proven. Opinions can be based on facts or emotions and sometimes they are meant to deliberately mislead others. Therefore, it is important to be aware of the author's purpose and choice of language. Sometimes, the author lets the facts speak for themselves.

Emotional, logical or ethical persuasion is neither right nor wrong, but the way in which it is used can be positive or negative. The more savvy and educated people need to teach and preach the practice of making reasonable judgement about the material in the media, and of drawing conclusions about the credibility of the texts, news, and reports. Facts or opinions will show -- if one judges objectively, and inspects both sides of an argument with an open mind.

(Originally published on http://www.aacs.website/wp-content/uploads/2018/11/AACSNL11.5.18.pdf)

16. The Imposition of Robot News

AI programs author news coverage across public and social media, many of them presented in the forms of news feeds based on the reader's location and personal preference. According to <u>Arun Vishwanath</u>, a Harvard University professor, "we will be presented with the version of the news we wish to read -- not the news that some reporter, columnist or editorial board decides we need to read. And it will be entirely written by artificial intelligence (AI)." The imposition of robot news becomes even more imposing because mindless readers tend to trust those news feeds on Facebook and Google News more than the credible, accountable, validated news sources, which also <u>employ machine-learning algorithms</u> to match us with news and ads.

As a result of the manipulation or imposition of what happens in the world, news reports will be influenced or directed by AI to formulate varied arguments and conclusions based on published opinions, not real facts. People's social media data, online shopping and browsing history will drive AI to present them with the news they would like to read. With such interference, a person's bias and ideology will be further reinforced and fortified to the extent that one may wonder whether individual journalism or independent perception of realities will be even possible.

For example, for a reader with strong views on gun control, news of gun violence and casualty might be presented from a certain standpoint where easy access of assault weapons leads to conclusions about how all purchase of guns can hurt the society. It will be a different story for another who seeks to preserve the Second Amendment rights of the people to keep and bear arms as part of the first ten amendments contained in the Bill of Rights. Other issues rather than gun regulations, such as mental healthcare or home environments, will be presented with data and conclusions questioning the validity of banning guns.

When the personalized, AI-driven reality is the only reality people experience, Professor Vishwanath worries that it will only project a "win-win for marketers, advertisers and readers -- but a giant loss for democracy as we know it, because it will take away the core of what makes democracies successful: well-informed citizens, who form opinions not by simply reading articles they agree with, but by examining that which they don't agree with -- and then finding common ground." All this benefits the advertisers and marketing companies, placing ads on the AI news feeds and web pages. To divert from that result, policy-makers must proactively prevent AI domination, limiting the extent to which algorithms access data, whereas the media should use self-regulation, implement valid journalism, and provide varied versions of news content. Most importantly, readers need to read/think critically, and seek information that is both agreeable and disagreeable, from online and offline formats, and thus formulate more informed views.

(Originally published on http://www.aacs.website/wp-content/uploads/2018/03/AACSNL3.4.18.pdf)

17. Just another Corporation Bankruptcy?

The oldest gun manufacturer in the US, Remington Outdoor Co., filed for bankruptcy in 2018 due to slumping sales. Established more than 200 years ago, the company's significant sales-drop came amidst demands for greater gun control in the US, as well as lawsuits stemming from the 2012 Sandy Hook Elementary School shooting, the Wall Street Journal reported.

A shooting at Marjory Stoneman Douglas High School in Parkland, Fla. that killed 17 people in February 2018, revived the debate on gun control, while hundreds of thousands of protesters took to the streets of US cities. Some US retailers raised the age limit for certain firearms purchases to 21 or stopped stocking semi-automatic weapons. Attorney General Jeff Sessions at that time proposed to ban bump stocks through regulations rather than wait for Congress to act, defying recommendations by federal law enforcement officials and subjecting the Justice Department to litigation from gun rights groups.

Is America's gun culture not as impregnable as it seemed? Does Remington's bankruptcy indicate the likely demise of gun enthusiasm? Or, are Remington's problems of its own making, including errors in financial statements and faulty products, leading to its fall more than outcry of gun protestors? The bankruptcy filing reported that Remington officials planned to hand over the reins to its creditors in exchange for writing off most of the company's debt. Cerberus Capital Management LP bought Remington for $118 million in 2007, assuming $252 million in debt in the process. Cerberus later formed a holding company called the Freedom Group Inc., consisting of Remington and other firearms manufacturers -- including Bushmaster, which Cerberus had purchased in 2006.

On the consumer side, Walmart and Dick's Sporting Goods have taken initiatives to eliminate sales of assault firearms. The FBI processed a record number of background checks on gun purchases during the election year in 2016, but the rate of background checks plunged following Trump's election. The slow and long path to reform gun laws might just have given way to yet another corporate protection. Remington would operate under Chapter 11, whereas strong gun control debate continues.

(Originally published on http://www.aacs.website/wp-content/uploads/2018/04/AACSNL4.2.18.pdf)

18. How Much Can the British Like the EU?

With Brexit heading towards an unending deferral, <u>NBC</u> News finds Europeans understand very little how EU works, other than expressing how they like it or dislike it.

The privilege of few borders, easy travel and free trade come in part because of the alliance. Out of a common goal for peace in a war-torn Europe 5 years after World War II, France and Germany devised a plan to avoid the two countries going to war again. Six nations reached a deal to pool their coal and steel resources in 1950. A treaty signed in Rome 7 years later formed the European Economic Community (EEC), which subsequently became today's European Union. The UK was one of three new members in 1973. Today the EU has 28 member states with a total population of more than 500 million, including Belgium, France, Germany, Italy, Luxembourg, the Netherlands, Britain, Ireland, Denmark, Greece,

Portugal, Spain, Eastern Germany, Austria, Finland, Sweden, Romania, Bulgaria, and Croatia.

Four institutions work together to run the EU: the European Commission, the European Parliament, the Council of the European Union and the Court of Justice. According to Treasury data, the UK contributed £8.5bn to EU in 2015. Each country receives money back from the EU to support development and other projects. The UK also gets a rebate, on its contribution, because much of the budget is spent on agricultural subsidies and the UK does not gain nearly as much as other countries like France. After all repayments were taken into account in 2015, Britain contributed about 12.6% of the entire EU budget. Germany paid the largest share, 21.36% and France was the second-biggest contributor at 15.72%.

Starting out as a trading bloc, the EEC promotes free movement of goods and services within the Common Market, and now advances its initiatives to encompass regional inequalities reduction, environment preservation, human rights support and education and research investment.

The EU is Britain's biggest trading partner. British citizens can work in any EU country. EU funding sponsors farmers, boosts job markets, redevelops poor areas, and supports research. The EU has made travel more affordable by challenging monopolies and creating competition. It has cut down the cost of mobile data roaming and set other living standards in Europe.

On the other hand, giving subsidies to farmers has led to surplus of some crops. The EU's regulations are costly to the British economy, and without its overpowering control, Britain would be more likely to establish trade relations with countries like China and India. <u>Some</u> believe Britain is being restrained by the EU, gains little for the money it pays in and would be better taking back control. Others opt for the benefits of staying in the EU. To this day, the conundrum of Brexit is still unfolding and has yet to be resolved.

(Originally published on
http://www.aacs.website/wp-
content/uploads/2019/04/AACSNL4.14.19-1.pdf)

19. Iraq's First Elections since Islam State Defeat

Iraqis voted in their first parliamentary elections on May 12, 2018, since the government defeated the jihadist Islamic State (IS) in 2017. According to BBC, 7,000 candidates from rival alliances vied for seats in the 329-member assembly. The incumbent Prime Minister, Haider al-Abadi, called on "all Iraqis" to take part in the elections and cast his ballot in Bagdad.

The competing coalitions were predominantly Shia or Sunni, though the Kurds had their own lists. Although the Shia-led government won praise for the victory over IS militants, many Iraqis were disillusioned by widespread government corruption and a slow economy.

Haidar al-Abadi, headed the Nasr list, which was considered to get the most votes. But under the Iraqi system he would not be able to form a majority government, and would have to negotiate for a coalition that could go on for months.

The veteran paramilitary commander Hadi al-Amiri headed the Fatah list, which had become the political home of the Shia fighters and supporters of the Hashd. On another front, Nouri al-Maliki, the former prime minister, captured Mosul and the Sunni territory.

Many Sunnis were worried about the Hashd fighters and their leader and candidate, Mr Amiri. Having close ties with Shias in Iran, Amiri would make the Iranians, through their friends in the Hashd, the strongest foreign force in Iraq.

Reuters reported that voter turnout appeared low, voter irregularities occurred, and three people were killed in an attack near a polling station in the northern province of Kirkuk, according to local media.

The elections came just days after US President Donald Trump abandoned the Iran nuclear deal on May 8, 2018. Some Iraqis feared their country could once again become entangled in any struggle between America and Iran. <u>Could Iran be the real winner?</u> Iran fought hard against the jihadist extremists. Many of Iraq's recovery efforts were also funded by Iran.

Iraq is fragile and battered since the Americans and their allies invaded in 2003. The country needed to have a chance to assume some stability through the elections. As a result in October 2018, the former Kurdistan Prime Minister, Barham Salih, was elected to be Iraq's president. Salih selected Abdul-Mahdi of the Shia party, to be the Prime Minister. Mahdi had 30 days to form a new government, facing major challenges of reconstruction, as well as needing to prevent the country from descending back into sectarian civil war. The elections produced a government all sects in Iraq could work with. After so many years of bloodshed, suffering and sectarian struggle, the elections marked a turning point for the country.

(Originally published on
http://www.aacs.website/wp-
content/uploads/2018/05/AACSNL5.13.18.p
df)

20. The Transformation of Kim Jong-un

After years of isolation on the global stage, the North Korean leader Kim Jong-un has emerged from an heir apparent <u>who orchestrated execution of his uncle and assassination of his half-brother</u>. He is becoming a skillful diplomat on the spotlight. The world witnesses his transformation from a spendthrift on hydrogen bomb and intercontinental ballistic missile testing to a connoisseur of political games. In due process, Trump, more than twice Kim's 34 years of age, has called Kim "short and fat," a "sick puppy" and a "little rocket man." And Kim has called Trump a "mentally deranged U.S. <u>dotard</u>," all the while formulating relations with China, Russia, Syria, South Korea and the US.

In April of 2018, Kim drove <u>a historic inter-Korean summit</u>, following co-staging of the Winter Olympics in 2017 with South Korea's

President Moon Jae-in. Pyongyang also proposed direct talks with the US, and ordered <u>a halt to nuclear and missile tests</u>, freed three US detainees, and <u>blew up its nuclear testing site</u>.

Thus, despite fiery rhetoric, brinkmanship and domestic despotism, the Trump-Kim <u>summit</u> was held on Singapore's Sentosa island on June 12, 2018. Vladimir Putin extended an invitation for Kim to Vladivostock in September and <u>Syria's President Assad said he would also like to visit Pyongyang.</u> Kim is stepping out as the delegate of a nuclear power and negotiating with world leaders from a strategic position.

This new diplomatic strategy embodies desire and necessity to strengthen and support North Korea's economy and modernization. To focus on economy after the completion of his weapons development, Kim needed to forge new and old coalitions.

China, North Korea's main trading affiliate and US's strategic partner, was the first country for Kim to realign. Kim's two visits to China in May 2018 happened days before he met the US Secretary of State Mike Pompeo. The trade talks with China's Chairman Xi paved the way for

North Korea to play US off against China and vice versa. China prefers staggered denuclearization and lift of sanctions to stabilize North Korea's economy.

Similarly, Kim used Moscow as leverage. Former North Korean spy chief Kim Yong-chol was on his way to the United States to deliver the "strangely large" letter to Trump for his "Supreme Leader." Meanwhile, Kim welcomed the Russian Foreign Minister Sergei Lavrov to Pyongyang. Coincidence or not, the frenemy relationship between Trump and Kim was at stake.

Syrian President Bashar-al Assad's relationship with Pyongyang is one that may also worry the US and the UN. North Korea established diplomatic relations with Syria in 1966 and sent troops and weapons to the country during the Arab-Israeli war in October 1973. Between 2012 and 2017, North Korea was reported to transport to Syria acid-resistant tiles, valves and pipes that could be used to make chemical weapons.

South Korean leader Moon has encouraged normalization of ties with North Korea via security and economic assurances, whereas Trump has recently revised his judgement of Kim, calling him "smart and gracious" and "very honorable." Seemingly, the whole world is being hoodwinked by Kim, while skeptics maintain that he is unlikely to yield his nuclear weapons, or relieve the grip of his repressive regime.

Proven to be a skilled or even beguiling statesman, Kim will hopefully phase out his own mystic masks and agenda to modernize his country and in time, become a stable, peaceful member of our global community.

(Originally published on http://www.aacs.website/wp-content/uploads/2018/06/AACSNL6.7.18.pdf)

21. What's He Doing in Asia?

As Donald Trump embarked on his historic trip to Asia in 2018, one could help but ask what he was to do in Asia. Resolving the security issues related to North Korea, expanding U.S. trade interests, or jeopardizing the region's peace as he had created uncertainty among Asian leaders in his first 10 months of presidency?

America's withdrawal from the <u>Trans-Pacific Partnership</u> (TPP) trade agreement had concerned policymakers and business leaders across the Pacific. However, Trump's <u>12-day itinerary</u> with bilateral and multilateral meetings in Japan, South Korea, China, Vietnam and the Philippines, was planned to accomplish the following, according to the Washington Post:

1) Clarifying U.S. Foreign Policy

Trump's "<u>America first</u>" vision could result in U.S. disengagement from the region. On the other hand, other than TPP, Trump had not deviated greatly from the Obama administration's "<u>Asia pivot</u>," which was devised to reassure allies about the continued U.S. presence in Asia. Commitment and partnership was anticipated.

2) Reinforcing U.S. Ties with Asia

Leadership in <u>Japan</u> and <u>China</u> took on an assertive role for the region as well as the globe. Prime Minister Shinzo Abe's was carrying TPP forward with the <u>11 remaining partners</u> in the absence of the United States. President Xi Jinping announced China's long-term vision of being a global leader. Trump was expected to strengthen his rapport with both Xi and Abe, as well as other Asian allies.

3) Forging a Consensus on North Korea's Nuclear Threat

With Moon, Xi, Abe and other leaders at the ASEAN meeting, Trump looked for allies and partners to "<u>strengthen the international resolve to confront the North Korean threat</u>" and move toward a denuclearized Korea.

4) Negotiating U.S. Trade Interests

Trump negotiated U.S. trade interests at the <u>APEC summit</u> in Vietnam. With Japan, Trump sought a bilateral free trade agreement (FTA), which would be at odds with Abe's hopes to keep alive the TPP deal. Trump also renegotiated the 2012 <u>KORUS FTA</u> with Korea, and addressed perennial trade issues with

China to lessen barriers to U.S. commercial engagement in the Chinese world.

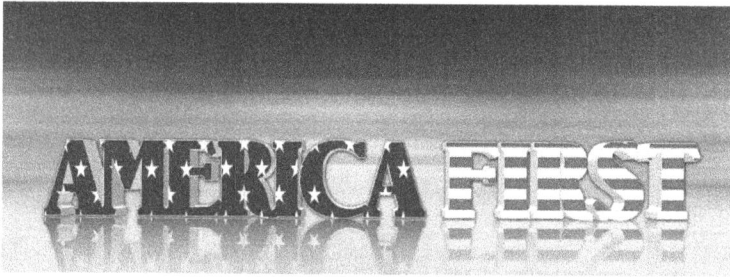

The 12-day, five-country trip, came at a precarious moment for Trump. His former campaign chairman was indicted, and another adviser pleaded guilty as part of an investigation into collusion between his 2016 campaign and Russian officials.

As Trump underwent domestic vulnerabilities, the trip presented a crucial international test. The White House proposed that Trump pushed American economic interests in the region, but the North Korean threat was expected to dominate the trip. The escalation of rhetoric undermined confidence in the U.S. as a stabilizing force in Asia.

The White House hoped the trip could offer a chance at a reset for Trump, an opportunity to forcefully assert U.S. pledges to its allies and send an effective warning directly to North Korea.

(Originally published on http://www.aacs.website/wp-content/uploads/2015/07/AACSNL11.8.17.pdf)

22. What Happens after

the 2019 Trump-Kim Summit?

The abrupt end to the February 2019 Trump-Kim summit in Vietnam shows both leaders' failed approaches via "big threats, big egos, and bad bets" as New York Time's journalists report. Without an anticipated deal on nuclear policies, liaisons, easing sanctions or peace affirmations, the world senses the setback looming larger. At the Singapore summit in June 2018, there was the hope of reconvening to sign a declaration of peace. Now that the confidence subsides, what happens next?

The North Koreans had been playing hardball ahead of the summit, hoping to lift sanctions. In exchange, they were willing to concede nuclear facility closures. Trump's unexpected departure from the negotiation table in the 2019 summit signifies a stance of taking no deals when the US demands are not met. Meanwhile, conflicting narratives seem to indicate the disparity of expectations has developed to hinder clear communications and understandings. Trump claims the North Koreans demanded sanctions to be lifted entirely; the North Koreans insist they only ask for partial easing of sanctions. Kim hopes to advance North Korea's economic goals and normalize relations with the US; Trump desires to see a denuclearized North Korea and advance his image/glory on the world stage.

The failed summit leaves the future of US-North Korean diplomacy uncertain. North Korea puts it out there that US is "missing an opportunity that comes once in a thousand years"; the US on the other hand, keeps the door open to further negotiations. NPR publishes an analysis by Professor Samore of Brandeis University that surmises "a blessing in disguise":

> Kim Jong Un will not abandon negotiations and will not resume nuclear and missile testing. First, North Korea has already made sufficient progress toward the development of thermonuclear weapons and long-range missiles so that a continuation of the moratorium on testing does not impose a significant technical

price.... A resumption of testing might provoke Beijing and Moscow to once again join Washington's campaign of "maximum pressure. A real deal may not be so far-fetched. There may be more developments to come inevitably.

Will North Korea move from the modest dismantling of Yongbyon nuclear site to a level of denuclearization acceptable to the global community? Will Kim, who gained spotlight through expansion of nuclear weapons, be willing to reduce or eliminate weapons of mass destruction? Will Trump exercise diplomatic prudence and work with his advisors and allies to seek the best courses of actions? What reciprocal actions will the US and its allies need to take to reach a real deal? These are the questions to ponder. Many factors and nuances of discourse will affect the outcome of these globally important negotiations. Deliberation, care and diplomacy is very much required.

(Originally published on
http://www.aacs.website/wp-content/uploads/2019/03/AACSNL3.3.19.pdf)

23. 2018-2019 American Government's Shutdown

December 22, 2018 while the world readied itself for the holidays, a standoff over Trump's $5.6 billion border-wall demand led to a partial government shutdown that has lasted into 2019. The shutdown became the longest of its kind in history. A spectrum of industries and workers were affected by this ongoing shutdown. 800,000 federal workers went months without pay. 25% of the US federal government had no funding. Nine departments' operations ceased, including Homeland Security, Justice, Housing, Agriculture, Commerce, Interior, and the Treasury. National Parks were closed. Major components of the U.S. immigration system, along with many government websites, were offline, out of order or under strain, the services "<u>unavailable due to a lapse in government appropriations.</u>" When federal agencies were dealing with migrant families crossing the border and crowding U.S. courts, the closure of the immigration authorities not only left workers unpaid, but frustrated many tourists and visitors.

In the front line, U.S. Border Patrol agents, Immigration and Customs Enforcement officers and other enforcement personnel at the Department of Homeland Security were working with merely an assurance they would be paid later; many of them were starting to call in sick. Still, more than 2,000 migrants per day on average added to their workload, according to the latest Customs and Border Protection statistics. With nowhere to detain these migrants, the government was releasing hundreds onto the streets in El Paso, Yuma, Ariz., and other border cities.

Consequences of the government shutdown also impacted the private sector. In addition to the approximately 800,000 federal workers who were either furloughed or working without pay, low-income employees such as cafeteria and custodial workers were out of work. Private companies with federal contracts were facing uncertainty.

Contractors' work, such as that of outsourced security companies, suppliers and researchers, was disrupted. Furthermore, IRS' closure meant tax returns and W-2 statements were put on hold -- which in turn, affected consumer spending.

After meeting top Democrats Nancy Pelosi and Chuck Schumer on January 4, 2019, Trump stated that he could continue the shutdown for <u>months or even years</u> to force funding of the US-Mexico border wall. He could also declare <u>a national emergency</u> to build his promised wall bypassing congressional approval.

Meanwhile, a search for a way out of the impasse was underway. Could resurrection of the old Democratic notion of pairing wall funding with DACA protections for the Dreamers put an end to the shutdown? Could Senator Lamar Alexander's idea of giving Trump an additional $1 billion to fortify ports of entry rather than a border wall be the solution?

The standstill remained until January 25, 2019, when Trump endorsed a stopgap bill to reopen the government for three weeks up until February 15 to allow for negotiations to take place. On February 15, 2019, Trump declared a national emergency in order to bypass the United States Congress, unsatisfied with a bipartisan border bill. To this day, the U.S. border security remains an issue, while a Congress deal averted another government shutdown.

(Originally published on http://www.aacs.website/wp-content/uploads/2019/01/AACSNL1.8.19.pdf)

23.   The U.S. Congress's Deal
on Border Security

A $1.3B border barrier spending was passed by the U.S. Congress in February 2019 and averted another government shutdown in America. CNN lists <u>what</u> entailed in the spending:

- $1.375 billion would cover roughly 55 miles of new barrier strategically placed -- including parts of the Rio Grande Valley, which had been a priority for the White House.

- The 55 miles was twice the amount allocated in the last spending agreement, but 10 miles less than the bipartisan Senate Homeland Security funding bill from 2018 that Trump rejected.

- The language and restrictions on the barrier itself were similar to what lawmakers had proposed in the past -- and had rejected by the President. This falls short of the 200 miles of steel-and-concrete wall/$5.7 billion that Mr. Trump demanded.

- Also, the deal prohibited the use of concrete walls. Only "existing technologies" for border barriers could be built. Bollard fencing was the most likely material to be used for any new barrier, aides said, but steel slats previously proposed, were technically an option.

- Democrats viewed detention beds as harsh and needlessly aggressive. Republicans viewed the detention beds as central to limiting the ability of detained undocumented immigrants from being released into the US as they await hearings. Immigration and Customs Enforcement (ICE) would provide enough money for 42,774 adult and 2,500 child beds with the goal of reducing that number to approximately 40,250 by the end of September 2019.

- The White House had the ability to move some money in the bill without a congressional blessing in order to provide more money for the wall or more detention beds. Thus, the total number of beds could go as high as 52,000, though there was no technical limit on the amount.

- The Democrats' demand for a cap on interior detention beds, at 16,500, was dropped in the final agreement.
- Overall spending for the Department of Homeland Security increased to $1.7 billion, primarily for technology, ports of entry security, customs officers and humanitarian aid.

The deal secured Trump's consent as he hinted that he had "'options that most people didn't understand' to build his border wall without congressional approval." Meanwhile, democrats and Republicans on the House-Senate panel showed willingness to compromise, not far apart on a plan to fund the Department of Homeland Security in order to boost personnel, technology and other efforts of securing the Southwest border.

(Originally published on http://www.aacs.website/wp-content/uploads/2019/02/AACSNL2.14.19.pdf)

25. What Happens When America Threats?

What happens when rhetoric fires up? More specifically -- when the American president and King Jong Un engage in heated verbal retorts? The bombing of Guam? Missiles on North Korea?

The current geopolitical tensions could threaten Asian growth, according to Richard Haas from the Council on Foreign Relations. Asia has been gaining economic success while no major wars impede its progress. Now, China's territorial aggression, North Korea's nuclear hostility, and the White House's stand under President Trump, all cause conflicts that could derail Asia's economic growth. Mr. Hass indicates that the factors that contributed to peace and stability in Asia "are now coming under increasing pressure."

Recent developments lead to conflict and disrupt Asian economic prosperity. Chinese demonstrations of sovereignty, about the Belt and Road Initiative -- President Xi Jinping's strategy is to make his country a global superpower. "As China adopts an increasingly assertive foreign policy -- exemplified by its border dispute with India, territorial claims in the South China Sea, and tighter controls over its own regions such as Xingjiang, Tibet, and Hong Kong, etc. -- other countries are increasingly motivated to boost their own military spending. As that happens, it becomes more likely that a disagreement or incident will escalate into a conflict," Hass writes. "The growing unpredictability of U.S. foreign policy could weaken deterrence and prompt allies to take their security into their own hands."

The Trump administration, facing the North Korean nuclear issue, has worsened the situation. While executing long-planned military exercises, America mobilized tens of thousands of American and South Korean troops. President Moon Jae-in of South Korea insisted that he holds a veto to any military action. "No matter what options the United States and President Trump want to use, they have promised to have full consultation with South Korea and get our consent in advance," he said. "The people can be assured that there will be no war." The North declared that as the military exercises begin, "the Korean

People's Army is keeping a high alert" and "will take resolute steps the moment even a slight sign of the preventive war is spotted."

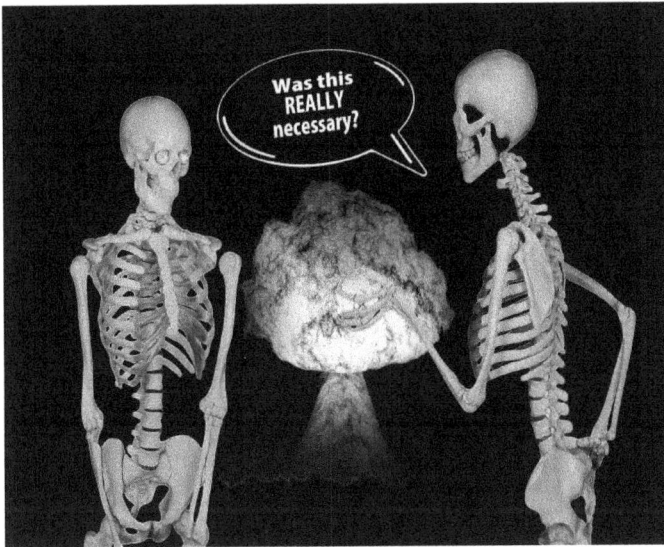

A pre-emptive strike or preventive war involves attacking first when an imminent attack is detected from a weaker rival. It is considered illegal under international legal conventions. Trump's national security officials are walking a tight rope, between curbing the bold threats that the president has tweeted and emphasizing that he is ready to act.

What is the consequence of Trump's threats and aggressions, you ask? A freeze of nuclear and missile tests in North Korea to delay the crisis, but not resolving it? Suspending progress on weapons, and all else! War or no war, Asia as a whole will suffer amidst the comebacks. Such military intimidation, executed or not, already has steep costs.

(Originally published on
http://www.aacs.website/wp-content/uploads/2015/07/AACSNL8.24.17.pdf)

26. A Checked and Balanced Future America

America is blessed with resources, wealth, economic power, military strength, freedom, civil rights, and liberties. This great nation, where people from round the world arrive to fulfill the American Dream, has however, been obscuring the vision its founders established for future generations. America, facing manipulation of fear and fixation to privilege, is relying on viable checks and balances to sustain democracy.

The midterm election in 2018 as well as the 2020 presidential election holds the keys to America's future. Will America stand clear of confusing political doubletalk to uphold its democratic principles? Will people vote for equality, or will they vote for privilege? In the midst of a #MeToo movement that seeks to punish sexual abusers, many powerful men elect to overlook outcries or protests against inequality. Whether the majority of people can vote for true equality or hold on to their own interest or privilege is crucial to America's future directions. The "election is not about policy or partisanship; it's about the principles of democracy."

Will the American republic remain a nation of the people, by the people and for the people? Will authoritarian populism prevail and become the new normal?

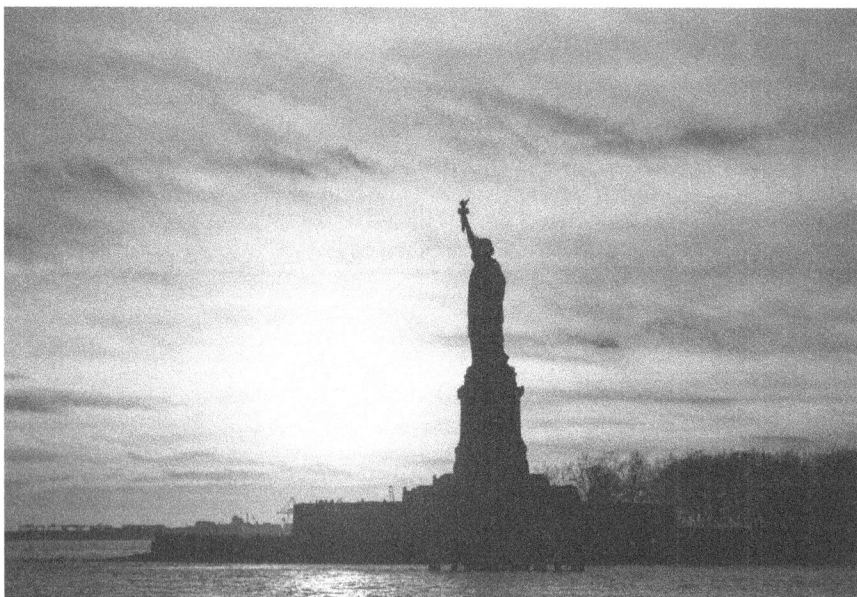

One would hope that democracy does not die from the rise of a demagogue. One would hope to elect wisely and stop the privileged from appointing and controlling the institutions and political parties that should otherwise resist authoritarian-style politics. Checks and balances should not become abstract theories or be sacrificed in practice. To give authoritarian brand of politics a stamp of approval is to disregard the downfall of a falling democracy.

History has taught the world this much: One cannot just roll the dice during elections and hope for a rectified society. Take a look at how ailing democracies died in Turkey and Hungary. When democratic principles are at risk, when the core tenet of democracy needs to be re-established -- citizens ought to be able to observe facts versus opinions and make informed choices to allow for a revival of a democracy.

Orwellian doublespeak and spineless kowtowing ought to be corrected; checks and balances ought to be exercised. Policies may divide the country; democratic principles must unite the nation. Redirect. Steer clear. Elect for checks and balances to take place.

(Originally published on http://www.aacs.website/wp-content/uploads/2018/10/AACSNL10.7.18.pdf)

27. Extradition of a Chinese Executive

Chinese telecom giant Huawei's chief financial officer and deputy chair, Meng Wanzhou, was arrested in Vancouver on December 1, 2018, to be extradited per US's request. While the U.S. has been investigating Huawei over violation of sanctions against Iran, President Trump did not receive any brief about the arrest prior. Meng, daughter of Huawei's founder Ren Zhengfei has been a prominent figure in the Chinese economy. Her arrest came at a sensitive time just days after Trump and Xi Jinping agreed to a trade war truce at the G20 summit end of November 2018. U.S. and China, engaged in a trade war, have imposed duties of billions of dollars on one another's goods lately.

China's embassy in Canada protested at the arrest and demanded Meng's release. Her detention occurred when she was changing planes -- the Chinese called it wrong-doing, while the U.S. justice department in the Eastern District of New York --

which Huawei said had brought the charges -- declined to comment. Subsequently at the bail hearing in Vancouver, the charges stated how Ms. Meng may have participated in a scheme to trick financial institutions into making transactions that violated United States sanctions against Iran. John Gibb-Carsley, an attorney with Canada's Justice Department, said that between 2009 and 2014, Huawei used a Hong Kong company, Skycom Tech, to make transactions with telecom companies in Iran, violating U.S. sanctions. Meng claimed Huawei operated in Iran in strict compliance with U.S. sanctions, and that Huawei's engagement with Skycom was part of normal business operations. She was granted bail by the Canadian court on December 11, 2018.

Meanwhile, western countries have been restricting the use of Huawei technology: U.S., Australia and New Zealand have blocked its equipment in infrastructure for new faster 5G mobile networks. BT, which dominates the UK's telecoms network, said it would not use the Chinese firm's equipment in its key 5G infrastructure. U.S. lawmakers have repeatedly accused Huawei of being a threat to U.S. national security, arguing that its technology could be used for spying by the Chinese government.

Notably Huawei is one of the largest telecommunications equipment and services providers in the world, recently passing Apple in smartphone manufacturing, second only to Samsung. The problem with Huawei is not only that they probably are pirating U.S. technology, but the fact that they are technologically advanced. Furthermore, they provide solutions that are affordable and thus are becoming a threat to the West.

If the purpose of the trade war is to attract talent/resources and gain economic advantages, western governments must create their competition edges. Detaining or extraditing executives with or without legitimate reasons will ultimately resemble building a wall around a country forcefully and impetuously. No real solutions to pirating or spying will likely materialize.

(Originally published on http://www.aacs.website/wp-content/uploads/2018/12/AACSNL12.13.18.pdf)

28. Interment of the Xingjiang Uighurs in China

An internment program that targets ethnic Uighur extremists in Xinjiang region of China has incarcerated one million in camps across the country's northwest. The so called "political re-education" camps are growing up to 1,300, although China denies detention of vast numbers of Uighur separatists.

Unrest in the area has a long history and is driven more by China's oppression of religious activity and preferential policies for non-Uighur migrants to the region. China has banned men from growing beards and women from wearing veils, and launched an extensive electronic surveillance program to erase a sense of Islamic or Turkish identity among Uighurs and other Muslim ethnic groups. The re-education programs, much akin to Communist China's pervasive cultural and political

117

propaganda, prohibit the detainees to pray, keep a copy of the Quran or fast during Ramadan.

According to former inmates and detainees' relatives, reasons for detention include traveling abroad, contacting or visiting relatives outside China, and having WhatsApp on their phones. Detainees have been reported disappearing after entering the camps, or died soon after they were released. Strict limits and surveillances are epitomized in slogans such as one sign at Turpan internment camp that reads: "Sense the party's kindness, obey the party's words, and follow the party's lead." Meanwhile, China declares that Uighurs enjoyed full rights but "those deceived by religious extremism... shall be assisted by resettlement and re-education."

Xinjiang is designated as an autonomous region in China, like Tibet to its south. Once at the intersection of ancient Silk Road trade routes, Xinjiang now threatens to become a black hole in President Xi Jinping's international "One Belt One Road" expansion effort. Amnesty International and Human Rights Watch have submitted reports to the UN committee documenting claims of mass imprisonment. The international community is taking note, while U.S.

lawmakers calling for sanctions. "[I]n the name of combating religious extremism and maintaining social stability," China has turned the Xinjiang region "into something that resembles a massive internment camp that is shrouded in secrecy, a sort of 'no rights zone'," Gay McDougall, a member of the UN Committee on the Elimination of Racial Discrimination, observed.

Whether or how the pushback from international human rights organizations will alter China's policies toward the Uighurs remains unclear. China continues to disguise the re-education regime as justifiable policy to centrally control Xinjiang. Its system of repression has <u>turned Xinjiang into a police state like no other.</u> In Hotan, "convenience police stations" are part of a "grid-management system." The authorities divide each city, village or town into squares, with about 500 people. Every square has a police station that keeps tabs on the inhabitants. At checkpoints, identity cards are scanned, photographs and fingerprints are taken, and newly installed iris-recognition technology is used to examine residents' eyes. Phones are confiscated for later data analysis. China imposes a police state to limit separatism and reduce violence. But by oppressing the Uighurs, the result is that the Xingjiang minority group is drifting towards more violence.

(Originally published on
http://www.aacs.website/wp-content/uploads/2018/09/AACSNL9.8.18-1.pdf)

29. Missing in China

As the world honors the labor force, commemorating the Chicago Haymarket affair in 1886, China impertinently shows its oppressive measures to eradicate any voice of protest or dissent. Six university students who wanted to work on May 1st/International Labor Day alongside regular laborers vanished in China. CNN tried to reach out to the missing students only to find that their phones were off. Missing persons and detentions of activists have become commonplace under oppressive schemes. Left-wing students have been detained across China because of their involvement in worker protests and demonstrations. Even those from Beijing's prestigious Peking University were blacklisted.

On May 4th, 1919, a student protest in Beijing set off a historic movement known as the May Fourth Movement, which objected the Treaty of

Versailles as an imperialistic humiliation, and subsequently marked the modernization of China. Upon the 100th anniversary of mass student protests against the former Republican Chinese government, how ironic it is to see disappearances of Chinese civilians. Even more notable is that "missing in China" occurs not only at this juncture, when student activism rises, but also has taken place in various parts of the country for quite some time.

China's minority Muslim Uighurs have been the targets of persecution in China. Xinjiang police use a mobile app to track citizens, and some of China's giant technology companies are associated with a mass surveillance system. Human Rights Watch noted that China's surveillance is sophisticated. The app uses facial recognition technology from a company affiliated with Alibaba Group Holding to match faces with photo identification and pictures on different documents. The app also takes other data points into consideration, monitoring electricity and smartphone use, as well as personal relationships to political and religious affiliations to flag suspicious terroristic activities.

The U.S. State Department says more than 1 million Uighurs are being held in camps in Xinjiang.

Human Rights Watch said that "data doors" at checkpoints are just means to obtain information from cell phones. The police app communicates with a database known as Integrated Joint Operations Platform, or IJOP, to collect data, file reports and prompt investigations. It provides a communication system for officials via voice, email and telephone calls, and uses Baidu map functionality for geolocation.

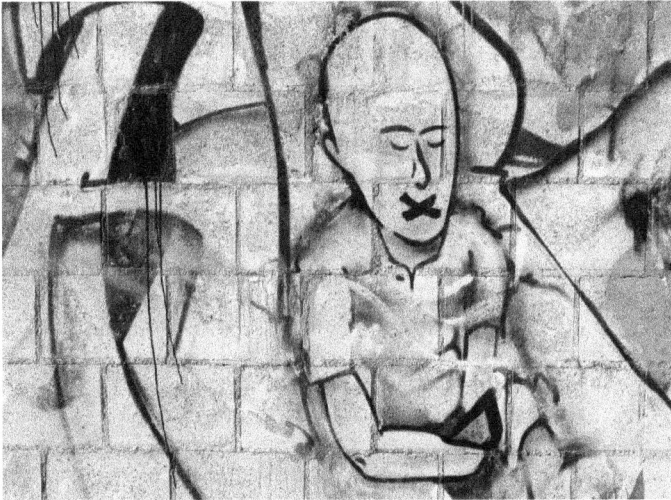

China has been criticized for its alleged detention of more than 1 million Muslims in

Xinjiang. Among various reports of physical and psychological abuse and forced labor camps, the UN has condemned <u>China's practice of racial and ethnic profiling</u> that disproportionately targets the Uighur community. It seems, though, the country needs to also curb its use of oppressive schemes across its populations.

(Originally published on <u>http://www.aacs.website/wp-content/uploads/2019/05/AACSNL5.10.19.pdf</u>)

30. Coming Together for Global Peace and Growth

In the process of examining world issues, one can discern that human conflict, inhumanity, climate change, and imbalance in allocation of resources construct the key factors that hinder world peace and growth. To tackle relevant challenges, the world needs to come together to make efforts for sustainable development and growth. Coming together implies that peoples are capable of viewing and positioning themselves as citizens of one global community.

The notion of a global community is of a vision affirmed by ancient seers, poets, and visionaries. The UN was formed after WWII in 1945, among many other world alliances and networks. Most notably, international humanitarian organizations, women's and youth movements, and individuals seeking to contribute and support world peace and growth have been emerging. Communication and information about the world as a community has become unprecedentedly efficient through advanced technology, news, and the internet.

The world is more interconnected than ever. However, world peace is still a work in process. Indeed, globalization of the economy benefits all, but the struggle among economic powers creates human conflict and severe inequality. People of all nations may proclaim their desire for world peace, but cooperation, collaboration, open and honest communication, and the redistribution of wealth, still leaves much to be desired.

How then, can the world come together? We could ban weapons of mass destruction, prohibit the sale of arms to waring countries and regions, coordinate and allocate resources, and squash crime/violation of human rights. We could not, however, deny peoples' basic instinct for self-preservation and self-interest. The key lies in each and every individual's ability to self-reflect, self-criticize, and stay self-reliant, which composes the root of global competence and global cooperation/collaboration. Self-awareness, curiosity, and desire to learn and grow, is the intrinsic transformation one needs to come together with the whole world. Extreme or unbridled nationalism is, then, an obstacle to world peace and growth, to the love of humanity as a whole. One needs to learn to acquire a birds-eye view to identify and realize the blind spot to world peace and growth: fear of others has far-reaching implications of incapability to grow and move forward as a planet.

In other words, inequalities concerning race, gender, and social/economic class, are the ultimate barriers to world peace and growth. Learning/ embracing differences and celebrating universality can keep the world moving forward while maintaining legitimate pride in one's own country and culture. Transparency and accountability can lead to justice and prosperity. When more people(s) become globally competent, the world may advance from struggling to resolve conflict to improving people's lives in environments of their own choosing. In turn, true freedom and harmony many be achieved for all.

"Think Global Live Noble" -- together we can build a better world!

Appendix

The Benefit of Diversity

The immigration issue fuels emotions as we have seen both in the recent political discourse and in the world throughout history. Many politicians such as Donald J. Trump find that their poll numbers rise the further from reality they drift. Republicans are far more certain than Democrats (53 percent versus 24 percent) that immigration is making our society worse.

As Ted Widmer affirms in the New York Times (Oct. 6, 2015), history provides some clarity about the relative costs and benefits of immigration over time. Fifty years ago Lyndon B. Johnson signed the Immigration and Nationality Act of 1965 at the foot of the Statue of Liberty. It made the United States a stronger nation. What ensued was arguably the most significant period of immigration in American history. Nearly 59 million people have come to the United States since 1965, and three-quarters of them came from Latin America and Asia. The flood of new immigrants promoted prosperity in ways that few could have imagined in 1965. Between 1990 and 2005, as the digital age took off, 25 percent of the fastest-growing American companies were founded by people born in foreign countries.

The 2010 census stated that more than 50 percent of technical workers in Silicon Valley are Asian-American. Google was co-founded by Sergey Brin, who emigrated from the Soviet Union with his parents at age 6. The C.E.O. of United Airlines is Mexican-American. And an extraordinary number of Indian-Americans have risen to become chief executives of other major American corporations, including Adobe Systems, Pepsi, Motorola and Microsoft.

In countless other ways, we might measure the improvements since 1965. A prominent AIDS researcher, David Ho, came to this country as a 12-year-old from Taiwan. Immigrants helped take the space program to new places, and sometimes gave their lives in that cause (an Indian-American astronaut, Kalpana Chawla, perished in the Columbia space shuttle disaster). Furthermore, American culture, in all aspects of music, art, cuisine, and others, became more interesting as it grew more diverse. A careful consideration of the 1965 Immigration Act shows that America's willingness to lower barriers made it a better country.

Lyndon B. Johnson signed the Immigration and Nationality Act on Oct. 3, 1965.

The Immigration and Nationality Act made America a genuinely New Frontier, younger and more diverse, truer to its ideals. On the other hand, it certainly increased American security from a more conservative standpoint. Significant numbers of immigrants and their children joined the United States military after 1965, and the armed forces became more ethnically diverse.

(Originally published on:
http://www.aacs.website/wp-content/uploads/2015/07/AACSNL11.111.pdf;
first printed in Asia-Literacy and Global Competence, 2017)

Study Questions for *The Un-death of Me*

One reader has suggested that reading my book *The Un-death of Me* was an exercise to become globally competent. I appreciate this observation of the reader, and confirm that my debut book and this collection of articles in *Global Competence Revisited* have similar purposes of examining the issues concerning cultural diversity and competence. I therefore, include as an addendum here, study questions for *The Un-death of Me*. In doing so, I hope to circle back to address some of the subjects I explore and elicit further discussions.

Discussion Questions for <u>The Un-death of Me</u>:

1. Do you think this "fictional memoir" is more fictional or autobiographical? To what extent is this book a cross-genre endeavor?
2. Does the book start in a disoriented way with a purpose? What purpose does it serve? Reflect on Avery/the protagonist narrator's state of mind and how "stream of consciousness" brings out her stories.
3. What kind of character is Harry? When Avery says she needs to teach people how she is to be treated, including adults and children, do you think she has this man and her students/step kids in mind? What other characters might be included in this list of people that need to be taught about cultural competence?

4. Do you think the character of Avery Mingli Liang is well developed? How has she changed throughout the book? What kind of realizations does she experience? To what extent is her isolation self-imposed? Does she establish true connections with her husband Abbey Lori? Or is it another quandary?

5. What kind of character is Tim Rosenberg? Abbey Lori? How are they similar or different? Why do you think these two men become the most important influencers on Avery's life?

6. Do you think you can be truly empathetic of Avery's immigration life and experience? Based on your own upbringing and heritage, can you picture what Avery has to undergo in order to find her niche in American society?

7. How sympathetic are you of people of foreign origins? Do you think they should all go home to avoid struggles in their adopted countries? Or, what do immigrant experiences like Avery's teach you?

8. What is your favorite part of the book? Why?
9. The differences and similarities among nations are nuanced in this book. Compare and contrast. Give examples.
10. The prologue/epilogue of the book draws out the same topic of quest and life fulfilment. To what extent do you think the implications change although they both employs very much of the same narration?

(First printed in <u>Asia-Literacy and Global Competence</u>, 2017)

Thank you for reading!

Dear Reader,

I hope you enjoyed the entries collected in *Global Competence Revisited.* In foregrounding every individual's level of global competence while investigating challenges or issues of our country as well as the global community, I aim to raise awareness about cultural diversity and sensitivity. In order to achieve true freedom and harmony of the world, one needs to have a base to explore the world far beyond. That is to say, one needs to embrace his or her culture and celebrate universality.

Global competence is the key to world peace and growth. My journey of learning continues and will never cease. I plan to keep writing about different facets of our global community. Our complex yet beautiful world has so much to offer, that it's hard not to explore as many aspects as our time allows us to.

Finally, I need to ask a favor. If you are so inclined, I'd love a review of *Global Competence Revisited*. Your honest review is the most precious feedback I could have.

You, the reader, have the power to make voices heard and change our world for the better. Please find below a link to my author page on Amazon: http://amazon.com/author/aliciasulozeron

Other platforms where you could communicate your thoughts about my book are as follows:

http://www.aacs.website/en/membership/featured
https://www.facebook.com/people/Alicia-Lozeron/100013834032346
https://www.facebook.com/aliciasulozeron
http://www.aliciasulozeron.com/

Please make yourself heard by voicing your opinions. Thank you so much again for reading. I look forward to reading your review.

Sincerely,

Alicia Su Lozeron

Global Competence Revisited

Global Competence Revisited

Author: Alicia Su Lozeron

About the Author

Global Competence Mentor | Founder of AACS | Author | Licensed Secondary-School English Language Arts and Chinese Mandarin Teacher | College English Adjunct Instructor

Think Global Live Noble

Alicia Su Lozeron is the author of numerous news/magazine articles, short stories, and novels. She holds a Master's degree in English and Comparative Literature from Columbia University in the City of New York, is licensed as a secondary-school English Language Arts/Chinese Mandarin teacher in the U.S, and serves as a college English adjunct instructor. Through her writing career as well as the communication management/travel consulting company she founded, Asia-America Connection Society, she aims to raises awareness about global competence, and to connect the world through global explorations and studies. <u>Asia-literacy and Global Competence</u> (2017) and <u>Global Competence Revisited</u> (2019), collections of her articles and vignettes, highlight her musings of cultural interactions and layouts the groundwork for her many endeavors. (See both English and Chinese versions at <u>https://www.amazon.com/Alicia-Su-Lozeron/e/B01N3LXBAN</u>).

Her debut novel, <u>The Un-death of Me</u>, depicts a world traveler and immigrant Asian American woman's life in a fresh light. It is a fictional world full of contemporary and global resonance; it is about many subjects: alienation, individuality, self-doubt, self-discovery, complexities of love and marriage, quests of fulfillment and happiness, (in)justice, cultural diversity, discrimination, and mankind as a whole. Its subtle yet intense emotions detailed in the many characters and locales, render a visionary sense of humanity, gratifying and unforgettable in their own rights. (See <u>https://www.amazon.com/Un-death-Me-Asian-American-Woman/dp/0998194123/ref=asap_bc?ie=UTF8</u>).

Alicia Su Lozeron
Asia-America Connection Society
Think Global Live Noble
Phone 702-505-9506
E-mail aliciasulozeron@gmail.com; info@aacs.website

Below is what readers and audiences have discerned of Alicia Su Lozeron's work:

• helps me overcome difficulties or fears and find beauty in positive human interactions;

• helps me appreciate people of various backgrounds, and expand knowledge about the world;

• helps me understand interracial or blended family relations;

• helps me savor intricate feelings and emotions about important subjects in life;

• helps me gain enjoyment through poetic narrations;

• helps me realize a new perspective of hope, courage, and respect for others;

• helps me raise awareness about cultural competence;

• helps me nurture a well-rounded global outlook;

• motivates me to promote an open/just community;

• urges me to develop the ability to see the big picture using multiple frames of references;

• helps me strengthen the ability to express genuine love;

• helps me decrease conflict by learning to trust and to resolve disagreements....

"Think Global Live Noble" -- together we can build a better world!

Detailed Information:
https://www.linkedin.com/in/alicia-su-lozeron
http://www.aliciasulozeron.com
http://amazon.com/author/aliciasulozeron
http://www.aacs.website/en/services/authors-and-books
https://www.facebook.com/aliciasulozeron
https://www.facebook.com/people/Alicia-Lozeron/100013834032346
http://www.aacs.website
https://www.facebook.com/aacs.website
https://twitter.com/AliciaSuLozeron

www.ingramcontent.com/pod-product-compliance
Lightning Source LLC
Chambersburg PA
CBHW061829260326
41914CB00005B/924